D0732331

No
Time to
Teach

The Essence of Patient
and Family Education for
Health Care Providers

Fran London, MS, RN

No
Time to
Teach

The Essence of Patient
and Family Education for
Health Care Providers

Fran London, MS, RN

Pritchett&Hull

Published by
Pritchett & Hull Associates, Inc.
3440 Oakcliff Road, NE, Suite 110
Atlanta, GA 30340

ISBN 978-1-933638-49-2

Manufactured in the United States of America

To my husband Jay

who brought me to Arizona which started me on this path of patient and family education.

Thank you.

Contents

Why teach?

Most health care is self-care.

Professionals provide only a small fraction of all health care.

After saving lives, the most important thing we provide is patient and family education. It promotes and supports the behavioral changes that improve health outcomes.

These behavioral changes may include:

- Taking medicine as prescribed
- Monitoring symptoms and responding appropriately
- Making and keeping follow-up appointments
- Regular exercise
- Eating the appropriate diet
- Choosing a safer and healthier lifestyle

A quote to ponder

"There is no prescription more valuable than knowledge."

— C. Everett Koop MD,

Former Surgeon General
of the United States

"I don't have time to teach"

By saying you don't have time to teach, your only solution is more time.

Your statement stops the process.

But, if you ask, "How can I most effectively and efficiently teach in the time I have?" you open yourself to the answer.

"How can I most effectively and efficiently teach in the time I have?"

Research shows the most effective and efficient way to provide patient and family education is to help the learner take part in the process and individualize your teaching to his or her needs.

Involve and individualize.

This book offers short cuts to providing quality patient education. Not quick fixes, but the shortest path to improve your patients' self-care skills.

At first, these shortcuts may not seem so short. This will change as you learn to focus your energies on efficiency and effectiveness. Other methods may appear quicker, but research shows they do not impact health outcomes as well.

For example, it may seem efficient to have brochures or educational TV in your waiting room. However, passive methods do not offer a good return on investment. They may increase knowledge, but don't impact actions often enough to be worthwhile.

However, if you transform these passive methods into active teaching methods, they can work. Greet the learner in the waiting room and say, "There's a good video coming on about flu shots. Please watch it, and we'll talk about it when you come back for your appointment." Or, hand the mom waiting with her sick toddler a booklet and say, "Here's a booklet on fevers in children. Please look it over and we'll talk about fevers later."

Effective and efficient teaching
Evidence to practice

Jahraus, D., S. Sokolosky, et al. (2002). "Evaluation of an education program for patients with breast cancer receiving radiation therapy." *Cancer Nursing* 25(4): 266-275.

The acquisition of knowledge is presumed to be part of coping with the stress of a breast cancer diagnosis. The purpose of this study was to evaluate the impact of an education program on the perceived adequacy of knowledge of patients with breast cancer receiving radiation therapy. Second, the intent was to investigate the patients' preferences regarding involvement in decision making, amount and type of information wanted, and preferred information-seeking activities.

Conclusions: Significant increases in perceived adequacy of knowledge scores indicate that the program was effective. Findings suggest that individual patients' information preferences, priority information needs, and preferred information-seeking activities should be identified early and incorporated within educational programs to target resources and maximize the likelihood that positive patient outcomes will result.

A frequently asked question

"Why don't we save time by having nursing assistants do some teaching?   They could teach simple things, like cough, turn, and deep breathe."

Yes, a nursing assistant could teach a patient to cough, turn, and deep breathe. But would he or she know why this is done? If asked, would he or she be able to fully explain it to the patient?

Patient and family education should be multidisciplinary. On the other hand, the most accurate and thorough teaching should be done by health care professionals who know the content, rationales and resources for additional information.

If you want health care team members who are not professionally trained to augment teaching, check their scope of practice and job descriptions. Then check yours.

Use assistants well, but don't abdicate your responsibility to teach. Non-professionals can still support patient and family education by:

- Identifying teachable moments, and alerting the appropriate health care team member in a timely manner.
- Promoting an environment that supports teaching, such as maintaining and stocking teaching tools.

A quote to ponder

A shortened hospital stay is justified in the best interest of patients, as the optimum location for a speedy recovery is at home with family and friends. The reality of what is happening, however, is that patients are often not prepared to provide the required level of self-care after an early discharge from the hospital.

— *Keeping,* 2002, page 70

Assessment

One step in teaching patient and family members that is often skipped is assessing their learning needs. Too often we jump right into teaching, without finding out first what the learner knows.

Why is it a mistake to skip assessment?

Assessment treats learners like adults.

Adults don't learn the same way children do, because:

- adults know stuff already
- adults know enough to get through life just fine
- adults only want to learn new stuff that will be useful

Adults want to be treated like adults, not like children. An adult with a chronic illness may know more than you about the diagnosis and the way he or she responds to treatments.

If we start teaching without finding out what the adult learner already knows, we:

- show disrespect, because we don't acknowledge what the learner already knows.

- bore and alienate the learner, because we teach what he or she already knows, or teach above or below his or her level of understanding.

A good learning assessment helps you teach more efficiently and effectively. If you just jump into teaching without assessing the learner, you may waste time teaching what the learner already knows. Or, you may present information in a way that makes the learner defensive or overwhelmed. When we alienate our learners, they don't pay attention to us and, consequently, don't learn. This wastes teaching time.

Assessment tells you what the learner knows, and helps you build a relationship with the learner. Both promote more effective teaching.

When you build your teaching on what the learner knows, it will make more sense to the learner. This will help him or her understand and remember the information better. If your learner reveals basic misunderstandings, assessment helps you identify and correct these.

If the learner's point of view is very different from your teaching, he or she will reject your information. You need to present your information in a way that is consistent with the learner's beliefs, so your learner can hear, understand and apply it. For example, someone who does not believe that germs cause illness may not apply your teaching about handwashing. The new information has to make sense to the learner.

Assessment lets you individualize your teaching so you can focus on the most important information and skills, and teach them in the most effective way. In practical terms, assessment is one way we apply adult learning theory to our clinical practice.

This is true whether you are caring for a patient with an acute or chronic illness. For example, before teaching about antibiotics, ask, "You said you have been taking antibiotics. What were they for?"

Assessment saves teaching time. The more your learner already knows, the less you have to teach.

Assessment
Real-life example

An adolescent with spina bifida kept getting readmitted with serious infections from skin breakdown on her legs. Each time she was discharged, she and her mother were taught about the need to change positions and how to watch for skin breakdowns and respond.

Yet she always returned to the hospital with new sores. Finally, a nurse asked her what caused the skin breakdown. She told the nurse the pathways in her home were too narrow for her wheelchair, so she got around the house by dragging herself across the floor.

The patient got a new, narrow wheelchair and this problem was solved.

A quote to ponder

The only man I know who behaves sensibly is my tailor; he takes my measurements anew each time he sees me. The rest go on with their old measurements and expect me to fit them.

— George Bernard Shaw

How to assess the learner

Assessment happens in conversation.

A full learning assessment tells you what the learner:

- believes
- knows
- expects
- misunderstands
- wants to learn
- is able to learn, and how
- is willing to learn

And how best to present the information so the learner understands and can use it.

You need to know where your learner is, and what he or she understands and believes. There isn't a set number of questions. Sometimes the answers to a few questions can give you a good sense of where the learner is. Sometimes you have no idea what is going on, so you have to keep asking more.

Use open-ended and non-leading questions as you talk with the learner. Ask in context. Let the conversation flow. Actively listen to what is and is not said.

An open-ended question cannot be answered with yes or no.

A non-leading question does not imply any preferred answer. Any answer is possible. For example, a leading question would be, "You don't smoke cigarettes, do you?" The non-leading version is: "Do you smoke cigarettes?"

Here are some questions that may help you get the information you need. Never ask them all at once at one sitting. Ask them within the context of the conversation to discover who the learner is, so you can best individualize your teaching.

To determine how he or she understands the illness and treatments (the learner's explanatory model) (Kleinman, Eisenberg & Good, 1978), ask:

- What problems have your illness caused for you?

- What concerns you most about this illness?

- What bothers you most about this illness?

- What do you fear most about your illness?

- What do you think caused the problem?

- Why do you think it happened when it did?

- What do you think this illness does to you? How does it work?

- How severe is your illness? How long do you think it will last?

- What kind of treatment do you think you should get?

- What are the most important results you hope to receive from this treatment?

These questions were adapted from Kleinman, Eisenberg & Good, 1978.

Kleinman's questions were designed to identify how best to approach patients and families whose culture or religion is different from yours. But they work for any patient. They help you to individualize your teaching for specific learning needs and provide culturally-sensitive care.

To identify the learning style that works best with this learner, ask:

- The last time you wanted to learn something, how did you go about it?

To identify the learner's priorities, ask:

- What do you need to know to take care of yourself at home?

- What do you want to learn more about?

Here are two multiple-choice questions to assess readiness to learn that are adapted from Austin & London, 2008:

To identify if the learner is ready for specific information, ask:

Some information might make people scared or worried. Which sentence best describes how much of this information you would want:

- I do not want to know anything that would scare or worry me.
- I am not sure if I am ready to hear anything that would scare or worry me.
- I want to know everything, even if it might scare or worry me.

To identify the amount of information to give at a specific teaching session, ask:

Which sentence best describes how you would like to receive this information:

- I want the simplest and least amount of information you can give me.
- I want to receive more than the simplest information.
- I want as much detailed information as you can give me.

These questions provide you with a range of information:

- readiness to learn
- emotional state
- motivation to learn
- language skills and literacy
- self-efficacy

- development
- physical and cognitive limitations
- sensory deficits
- culture
- religion
- financial limitations

These are not the only assessment questions. Let the answers guide you.

The information you gather in these conversations will be used to modify your teaching and methods. Keep asking questions to get a sense of how well he or she understands, and how much information to give.

Assessment makes teaching more effective

It's not just what you do with the assessment findings that help you teach better. Assessment enhances learning. Researchers (Doak, Doak, & Root, 1996) discovered an interesting twist when they evaluated the effectiveness of specific teaching materials. They found that by doing a pre-test before teaching, no matter what the tool was, the learners learned better.

Why?

A pre-test sets up the learner. Even if the learner does not know the answer at the time of the pre-test, it prepares the learner to look for the answer. Then, when you teach it, the learner notices that information and remembers it. And when you give the post-test, the learner knows the right answer. So the pre-test makes your teaching more effective by preparing the learner to learn. This technique is called an advance organizer.

This doesn't mean you should actually test your learners before you teach. In the context of providing health care, knowledge tests are not appropriate. You want to develop a therapeutic relationship that promotes healing. Tests are threatening because they reveal weaknesses and make failure possible. They increase the learner's anxiety and alienate the learner by creating an environment that feels unsafe. This is not helpful.

Instead, just by having a conversation to assess learning needs, you prepare your learner to listen for the information you present. For example, before you teach, ask your learner if he or she ever knew anyone with a central line before, or saw a dressing change. Even if the answer is no, the learner will be primed to pay attention.

Knowing how your learner understands helps you individualize your teaching

It may seem that if you skip the assessment of learning needs and jump right into teaching, you save time because you're doing less. However, this is not true.

If you skip the assessment, you risk harming the therapeutic relationship, and wasting time by teaching what the learner already knows, disagrees with, or is incapable of understanding. Your assumptions can waste time if you continue teaching in a direction that is not productive.

Assessment gives you the information you need to individualize teaching, it helps you build your relationship with the learner so teaching is more effective. Assessment is the ultimate teaching timesaver.

The best patient and family education supports patient-centered care and family-centered care. You cannot center your care around them if you do not know where they are.

Build relationship through assessment Real-life example

A nurse practitioner in a women's clinic was assessing a 33-year-old patient. The patient said that she was not married but sexually active and not using any contraceptives. The nurse practitioner warned the woman she may have been safe so far, but she was putting herself at risk. The more the nurse lectured her about contraception, the more the patient's eyes glazed over.

Finally the nurse asked the patient why she wanted to risk unmarried pregnancy and STDs. The patient said, "I don't need contraception. I have sex with a woman."

Individualization of teaching
Evidence to practice

Koelling, T. M., M. L. Johnson, et al. (2005). "Discharge education improves clinical outcomes in patients with chronic heart failure." *Circulation* 111(2): 179-85.

Although interventions combining patient education and post-discharge management have demonstrated benefits in patients with chronic heart failure, the benefit attributable to patient education alone is not known. We hypothesized that a patient discharge education program would improve clinical outcomes in patients with chronic heart failure.

Conclusions: The addition of a 1-hour, nurse educator-delivered, teaching session at the time of hospital discharge improved clinical outcomes, increased self-care measure adherence, and reduced cost of care in patients with systolic heart failure.

Frequently asked questions

Could I just hand the patient these questions, printed on a questionnaire, and ask him or her to fill it out?

A questionnaire sounds like a more efficient use of time ("fill this out in the waiting room") but won't give you the detailed information you need.

Assessment through conversation is most direct and accurate.

The purpose of the assessment is to give you insight into who the learner is. You need to get a sense of how to frame your teaching, how much detail the learner needs, and how best to present it. This is done best in conversation, observing the learner's responses, and listening to what is said and how it is said.

Problems with a questionnaire include:

- Open-ended questions would require

paragraphs of response, and you may not be able to read the handwriting.

- Those with emotionally sensitive concerns may not be able to adequately communicate them in writing.

- Those with poor literacy skills could be alienated by being asked to read and write.

- Since you would still need to have a conversation with the learner, no time is being saved.

Think about it. If you have a written questionnaire that asks, "What kind of treatment do you think you should get?" the patient may respond, "You're the doctor. You tell me." Yet sometimes, in conversation, this may be exactly the right question to ask in order to understand why your learner is having trouble following directions.

Why should I gather information in the assessment to individualize teaching to the learner's specific needs? If I have to teach all patients with high blood pressure about their medicines, wouldn't it be more efficient if I had a set list of things to teach and taught them to all my patients in the same way?

The information from the assessment tells you where to start teaching.

Assume your patient has high blood

pressure, despite prescribing increasing doses of medication. The first thing to find out: is the patient taking the medicine? If not, why not? You may learn the patient doesn't feel sick, so he doesn't believe it is important. Or doesn't have money to fill the prescription. Or thought that when you "took his blood pressure" you removed the problem. The assessment tells you what to teach, and how. If, instead, you just jump into your blood pressure teaching checklist, you will waste a lot of time.

Assume a woman who had a heart attack refuses to go to cardiac rehab. Without assessment, you may lecture her about recovery from heart attacks, which may get you nowhere. Instead, ask what she knows about cardiac rehab, and why she isn't interested in it. She may say she doesn't have transportation. She may tell you her neighbor died of a heart attack right after a rehab session. Or she may tell you she's not an alcoholic, and doesn't need rehab. The answer you get tells you how to tailor your teaching so it works with this learner.

Have a conversation with your learner. Listening helps you learn how to teach and how to present your teaching. If you use the words, expressions and imagery your learner uses, your message will connect better. Your learner will understand quicker.

All this saves teaching time.

It is most effective and efficient if you involve the learner in the process and individualize teaching to the needs of the learner. Teach in response to teachable moments. A checklist of topics to teach can be used as a reference, but not as a guide to structure your teaching. You may review the list occasionally to be sure you discussed important issues relating to self-care skills or how to recognize problems and respond. But if you teach from it, you are teaching from your agenda, and not teaching to your learner's needs.

A frequently asked question

"Do I need to know the beliefs and practices of my patient's ethnic group to provide appropriate education?"

No. To teach appropriately, you should know the beliefs and practices of the specific learner.

Even if you know the beliefs and practices of a particular ethnic group, unless you assess your learner directly, you will not know where your learner is right now. When cultures mix, they mix dynamically and on a continuum. You cannot predict which parts of the old culture a person would keep, and which parts of the new culture that person would adapt. Some may speak their native language at home, but English when they're out. Others may not. Some may see both traditional healers and allopathic health care providers. Others may not. So just knowing about an ethnic group doesn't tell you what a specific patient believes and does.

There is a danger that if you focus on learning about a culture, you will stereotype your learners. This can interfere with developing a therapeutic relationship. Instead, try to learn more about the person at hand, and hone in on the issues you need to consider when individualizing teaching.

If you teach enough people from the same ethnic community, you will, over time, understand their range of beliefs and practices. Then you may develop specific questions about the culture, and you may turn to literature and your resources in that community to get answers. This process is part of your professional growth and development.

From this knowledge, you may develop some assessment questions to ask members of a specific group, such as asking a patient if she follows halal dietary laws. When used appropriately, this will add content to your assessment and enhance the therapeutic relationship.

When you teach, focus on listening to your specific learner and learning his or her story.

A quote to ponder

"For many ethnic groups, spiritual and natural forces can cause illness, and treatment should be based on those beliefs. When these differences are not addressed in the clinical encounter, the consequences can be noncompliance and misunderstandings."

— Taylor, 2005, page 137

Listening

Here are some features of good listening skills.

- Want to listen.
- Tune out distractions.
- Listen to the whole message.
  Don't interrupt.
- Listen actively. Hear what is being said and think about it.
- Be interested, don't just show interest.
- Listen on many levels. Listen to what the speaker is saying and what that tells you about him or her.
- Listen for meaning. Listen for what isn't being said, too.
- If what the speaker says arouses your emotions, don't focus on your reaction. You will not be able to listen.

- Don't tune out your feelings, but let them be a cue to pay attention. The speaker's words trigger something in you.

- Listen for the speaker's feelings. Refer to feelings with the same words the speaker uses.

- Read gestures and body language, such as body position, tone, and breathing.

- Repeat important points to the speaker to make sure you understand.

- Silence is OK. It helps you or the learner collect thoughts or emotions, review what was said, or decide what to talk about next.

- Speakers repeat themselves when they feel they were not heard. If this happens, clarify that you heard and understand the meaning so the speaker can move on.

A quote to ponder

All you have to do is listen — really listen.

— Dass and Gorman, 1985, page 69

Listening
Real-life example

A mother brought her 6-year old son into the emergency department at three in the morning because he had ringworm of the scalp. He had the small local infection for several days, and she wanted him treated immediately.

The triage nurse and doctor considered her an emergency department abuser. They wondered why she got her son out of bed at three in the morning for a routine exam.

But there were logical reasons. The mom works the late shift at a nursing home and got off at 11:30 at night. It took her four bus transfers to get home by two in the morning. On the table was a note from the child's teacher saying he won't be allowed back in school until his scalp was looked at by a doctor. The mom gets public assistance that is tied directly into her child's school attendance, so this was an economic emergency for the family. The mom felt that she was a good mother for bringing him to the hospital immediately.

Teachable moments— When to teach

Teachable moments are points in time when the learner is open to new information. To identify teachable moments, notice when:

- the learner asks questions or provides information
- the learner talks about a problem he is having
- you are or the learner is performing a skill or providing a treatment
- the learner sees something on television that relates to his or her situation
- the learner expresses a need for change
- the learner complains of a lack of support
- the learner appears interested
- the learner appears misinformed on a topic

You are teaching more effectively and efficiently when you teach specific information when the learner is ready to hear it. When you work with teachable moments, you don't have to struggle to get attention or keep interest. You are giving them what they want when they are ready for it.

Here are some examples of teachable moments:

- Describe the procedure you are doing. "I'm putting the antibiotic in the IV."

- Explain why you are doing something. "I'm wearing gloves so the germs from my hands don't get on the incision."

- Address something you observe in an interaction between a patient and visitor. "If you leave the side rail down, he could roll out."

- Tell a patient what to expect in the upcoming test or procedure. "Before the test, you will get some medicine to make you sleepy."

- Reassure with information. "Oh, the needle doesn't stay in your arm! See, the IV catheter is made of a flexible plastic."

- Provide anticipatory guidance. "Your baby won't be able to sit up by himself for another month or so. His muscles have to develop."

Teaching, literally, begins at admission. It is more effective to spread teaching out in small pieces that build on one another over time. Involving the learner in the process saves teaching time because you get immediate feedback that keeps you focused on the most important issues. The information has time to be integrated and applied, and the learner will have opportunities to ask questions as they come up.

Some topics to be taught are not known until the discharge orders are written, like discharge medications. But during care, you can teach about the signs and symptoms being treated, the treatments, and the indications that something is going wrong. Provide anticipatory guidance. Then, when discharge orders are written, only the specifics are new. The learner will already know the context and rationales.

Every member of the health care team has an opportunity to identify and take advantage of teachable moments with every interaction with the patient and family. If most of these moments are taken advantage of, there can be enough time to complete all the teaching necessary for a safe discharge.

Teachable moments
Evidence to practice

Winickoff, J. P., V. J. Hills, et al. (2003). "A smoking cessation intervention for parents of children who are hospitalized for respiratory illness: The Stop Tobacco Outreach Program." *Pediatrics* 111(1): 140-145.

Parental smoking is associated with increased rates and severity of childhood respiratory illness. No previous studies have examined child hospitalization as an opportunity for parental smoking cessation. We evaluated the feasibility of implementing a smoking cessation intervention for parents at the time of child's hospitalization for respiratory illness.

Conclusions: This study demonstrates the feasibility of engaging parents in smoking cessation interventions at the time of child's hospitalization for respiratory illness. Previous work done in a similar sample of parental smokers has shown extremely low "ever-use" rates of cessation programs. High rates of acceptance of in-hospital and telephone counseling in this study support the notion of child's hospitalization as a teachable moment to address parental smoking.

A quote to ponder

"It takes experience and resources to develop the teaching skills of the bedside nurse, so that those teachable moments are easily recognized and suitably used to give patients and family members valuable information in small doses."

— Palazzo, 2001, abstract

What to teach

It is often said you should teach the "need to know" and not the "nice to know." But how do you know what the learner needs to know?

Your assessment of the learner's needs will inform you of some of the content the learner is not yet familiar with, or misunderstands. But where do you begin?

The most important content, the need to know, can be defined by the short-term goals of patient education.

Every learner needs to:

- Make informed decisions
- Develop self-care skills to survive
- Recognize problems and know how to respond
- Get questions answered

The long-term goal of patient and family education is to promote improved self-care behaviors to optimize health outcomes.

Think about what each learner is facing.

- What questions does the learner have?
- What decisions does the learner have to make?
- What self-care skills does the learner need to survive?
- What problems may occur at home?
- How can the learner recognize them early, and how should the learner respond?
- Who should the learner turn to for continuing care?

The answers to these questions, as well as your assessment findings, define what you should teach.

What you teach is guided by the goals (informed consent, self-care skills, recognizing problems and knowing how to respond, and questions) and your assessments. What is essential for this learner to know now to be safe? Above all, everyone needs to know who to call with questions, concerns, and for follow-up.

A frequently asked question

"How much information about side effects of medications should I give patients? I want them to be informed, but not confused."

How do you teach enough, but not too much? Use conversation, interaction, and assessment. Start with the most important information, so if the learner expresses discomfort or distress, you can stop.

Make sure the learner understands:

- the purpose and administration of the medication
- the risks involved
- how to recognize problems
- how to respond

How to teach

In today's busy health care system, there is little time for formal teaching sessions. Fortunately this is not a problem, because formal teaching sessions are not the most effective and efficient way to teach.

The best way to involve the learner and individualize the teaching is to teach informally, in conversation.

First, set the expectations.   Discuss with patients and families their role in continuing care, and that optimal health outcomes depend on their collaboration with the health care team. Tell them teaching will take place in every encounter through conversations that may seem informal, and questions are always welcomed. Tell them some of the interventions done in the hospital they will need to do at home.

Since most health care is self-care, encourage learners to know the answers to the "Ask Me 3" questions:

- What's my problem?
- What do I need to do?
- Why?

These questions acknowledge their right to ask questions and their responsibility in the relationship with the health care team.

Posters and brochures are available to reinforce this at: www.askme3.org

In order to prioritize your teaching, identify first what the learner understands and what the learner wants and needs to know. Before you can teach, you need to assess. Then, use the information you gathered in the assessment to plan your teaching. Collaborate with the learner to set goals, negotiate, and prioritize. The first priority is always to answer the learner's questions.

Teach in context, in the teachable moment, when the learner is ready to hear a bit of information. For example, tell the learner about a medicine as you are giving it. Describe the side effects or adverse reactions you are watching for. Then, upon discharge, as you provide each prescription, review the details and administration of each medicine. Discuss how medication administration fits into the lives of the patient and family.

When teaching a manual skill, like a dressing change or medication administration, plan brief but focused teaching sessions. Ask permission to turn off TV, radio, and video games during this conversation.

Then build on these steps:

1. Tell the learner what you are doing as you demonstrate the entire skill.

2. Demonstrate each step in detail.

3. Have the learner demonstrate with help.

4. Have the learner demonstrate without help.

Then, with breaks of hours or days, have the learner demonstrate the skill without help at least 3 times. This will increase the chances that something will go wrong, and reveal the learner's ability to problem-solve.

Review and reinforce vital information often.

Individualize your teaching by choosing the right teaching tools to meet the learner's needs. If the learner will have to perform the skill at home, he or she may need a reference to refer to with the details. This may be a booklet, pamphlet, or tear sheet. If one does not exist, have the learner take notes when you demonstrate the skill. These notes will be directions the learner can follow at home.

Be patient with your learning curve. Despite the fact that patient and family education is essential to a successful health care system, and it requires a complex set of skills, it is not emphasized enough in the education of health care providers.

Your skills will improve through the interaction between your awareness and experience. Just doing something doesn't make you better at doing it. Improvement is the result of paying attention to how you do it, what results you get, and the adjustments you make in response that give you a better outcome. Increase your awareness of when and how you teach by paying attention, and asking questions. Experience will help you see patterns so, over time, you will begin to recognize cues.

For example, some health care providers insist they have never had patients with low health literacy skills. Yet the incidence of low health literacy would make that unlikely. The more aware you are that low health literacy exists, the more likely you will notice a learner's cues.

So be persistent and be patient. Awareness and experience will improve your ability to provide high quality patient and family education.

Written discharge instructions are not enough
Evidence to practice

Logan, P. D., R. A. Schwab, et al. (1996). "Patient understanding of emergency department discharge instructions." *Southern Medical Journal* 89(8): 770-775.

Patients were interviewed immediately after discharge outside the emergency department to determine whether they could read their discharge instructions and recall their diagnosis and treatment plan. The association between frequency of correct responses and various characteristics of the patients was assessed.

Of the patients completing the interview, 72% could read the discharge instructions. The illiteracy rate was higher for patients with less than 9 years of education and for patients aged 50 to 59 years. There was no association between patient race, sex, or literacy. The correct diagnosis was given by 79% of patients, correct treatment information by 49%, and correct follow-up information by 82%.

Overall, 37% of patients answered all questions correctly and 8% answered all questions incorrectly. No association was found between frequency of correct responses and variables examined. Miscommunication of discharge information occurs frequently; illiteracy does not completely account for the observed low rates of recall.

A quote to ponder

"Things that matter most must never be at the mercy of things that matter least."

— Johann Wolfgang von Goethe

A frequently asked question

"What do I do if the patient asks a question I don't know the answer to?"

If the question is in your scope of practice, but you don't know the answer:

1. Tell the learner you don't know the answer, but will find out and get back to him or her.

2. Find the answer.

3. Get back to him or her.

If you can't answer the question because it is in the scope of practice of another health care professional or clergy:

- Tell the learner that is a very good question, but he or she has to ask the appropriate person.

- Give the learner a pen and paper to write down that question to ask it later.

- If there is some urgency to the question or if the learner requests it, offer to call that professional to speak to the learner.

If no one knows the answer (such as, "will I lose my leg?"), tell the learner no one on the health care team can predict the future. Invite the learner to discuss his or her fears, worries, or feelings ("It sounds like you're concerned that you could lose your leg . . .").

Always respond to a question in some helpful way. Do not ignore or make light of a learner's concerns.

Active Involvement

Adults learn best through active involvement. Interaction shortens teaching time. When you teach interactively, you continuously observe and evaluate the learner's responses. This helps you fine tune your teaching to the learner's needs.

When people actively interact with information during the learning process, a chemical change takes place in their brains that enhances learning and memory. Involve the learner by creating sensory connections. For example, when teaching a learner to hook himself up to an IV, have him note the smell of the alcohol swab as he or she is using it. When we learn, the thoughts, muscles and feelings all connect and learn new ways to respond. The more pathways new information makes into the brain, the more connections and associations it makes. The more associations it makes, the more ways the information can be recalled.

For example, did you ever hear an old song and remember the details of your life when that song was popular? These are associations. You used the music association pathway, your brain's cross-referencing system. You could have also brought back that same time of your life if you thought, "What was I doing in 1991?" This uses a different pathway for recall.

Have the learner apply the new information right away so the connections are strengthened. For example, after giving a patient a prescription for an antibiotic and providing the associated education, ask, "What should you do with the leftover pills?" The patient should apply the new information and state that there will be no leftover pills.

The simplest and most direct way to actively involve the learner is in conversation. This can be used to both involve the learner in the process and individualize teaching to the needs of the learner. Lead the conversation from the familiar to the new. For example, a patient going home with a cast may be asked:

- Did you know you'll be going home in a cast?

- Have you or anyone in your family ever had a cast before? What kind of cast was it? Tell me how you took care of the cast.

- Do you know what your leg will look like when the cast comes off?

- What bothers you about the cast?

- What worries you about having a cast?

Each question helps you individualize your teaching to the needs of the learner. Inject bits of information, as appropriate, and teach within the conversation.

With a little effort it is easy to transform passive involvement, such as reading, watching a video, or thinking of an answer to a question, into active involvement. Just add:

- **Conversation**. Ask the learner to describe the message in his or her own words.

- **Writing**. Have the learner write down the answer, take notes, or circle information on a handout. Ask the learner to write questions or concerns.

You can also create learning activities that actively involve the learner. Here are some examples:

- **Arrange the photos game**. Take photos of steps in a self-care skill, such as a dressing change. Give the learner the photos and ask him or her to arrange them in the order they are done. Then ask the learner to use the photos to talk you through the steps. This method can also be used with learners with low literacy skills.

- **Sort true and false statements**. This technique is useful for topics many people misunderstand. Identify key facts and misconceptions about a subject. Print the statements on heavy paper. Cut the statements into individual strips. Label one full piece of paper "true" and another "false." Ask the learner to sort the strips on to the appropriate piece of paper. For example, if the subject is AIDS, one statement may be "I can get AIDS from shooting heroin" and "I can get AIDS from donating blood." Discuss the results.

- **Sort problems and responses**. This is useful if you work with a patient population that experiences the same set of side effects and potential complications, such as those undergoing chemotherapy. Identify key signs and symptoms that may occur. Print these on heavy paper. Cut them into individual strips. Label one full piece of paper "Call your health care team on the next business day" "Call the physician on call right away" and "Call 911." Have the learner sort the signs and symptoms on to the paper with the appropriate response. Discuss the results. This activity can build the learner's confidence if you have many signs and symptoms that are easy to assign to a category.

- **Sort topics to review in order of importance**. This is useful if you work with a chronically ill patient population. Identify key topics that might be useful to discuss. For example, those with chronic renal failure may be interested in learning more about itching, cramps, mouth odor, depression, sexual dysfunction, diet, or medication. Put each topic on one index card. Ask the learner to sort them into what he or she would most like to talk about on top, down to the least important topic on the bottom. Use the results to prioritize teaching that day.

Use your creativity to design activities appropriate for your learners. Use your assessment and awareness of the learner to apply them. Some activities may be inappropriate for cultural reasons. In some situations the wife is the patient, but the conversation needs to be with the husband. For learners with lower literacy skills, use activities that involve objects or pictures.

Functional health literacy

Functional health literacy is the ability to read, understand, and act on health information. This includes reading and understanding prescription labels, interpreting appointment slips, filling out health insurance forms, following instructions for diagnostic tests, and understanding other health-related materials with information patients need.

Some people who function quite well (such as those who have a job and drive a car) have low health literacy. This means their ability to read, understand, and act on health information is impaired.

Functional health literacy can be worse than one's general literacy, because the health information may have vocabulary and concepts that are totally new to the learner. Even well educated people can have times when they do not understand health information, making them functionally health illiterate.

When a patient or family misses appointments, doesn't fill or use prescriptions as ordered, or appears to refuse to follow medical advice, low functional health literacy could be the cause. People with low health literacy skills have an incomplete understanding of their health problems and treatment, have worse health, and are at greater risk for hospitalization and death. They may not understand what they are expected to do, and may not be able to follow written instructions.

If you suspect a patient or family member has low functional health literacy, here are some interventions to help him or her get the most out of the health care encounter:

- Create a shame-free environment that makes the patient or family member feel safe and welcomed.

- Use simple and direct language and give examples when teaching. Clarity is not the same as talking down. The difference is in the attitude. If a person overhears your conversation and thinks you're talking to a child, you're talking down. Instead, explain it clearly without a condescending tone. Think, "I'm not being clear enough" instead of, "You're not smart enough to get this."

- Use the "teach back" or "show me" technique to evaluate understanding. Ask, "I may not have been very clear when I explained that. Could you tell me what

you heard, so I can be sure I did that well?"
If necessary, reassess and re-teach.

- Ask them to invite a family member
  or friend to the health care encounter.
  A support person can hear the same
  information, and help them understand
  or apply it.

Functional health literacy
Real-life example

An 81 year old, who has had several heart attacks, went to the emergency room for incapacitating knee pain from her osteoarthritis. The nurse who discharged her told her to eat a "regular diet."

The woman was so excited when she got home, she called her daughter. She didn't have to do that low fat, low sodium diet anymore! They told her she could eat regular food again! How she missed potato chips!

A quote to ponder

The chief virtue that language can have is clearness, and nothing detracts from it so much as the use of unfamiliar words.

— Hippocrates

Functional health literacy
Real-life example

A woman had a heart valve replacement. She lived in a small Midwest town with only one doctor, and that one doctor was from India. The woman didn't like him. She had trouble understanding him and thought he was trying to kill her. There was no other doctor she could go to.

Her neighbor told her the coumadin she was taking was rat poison. The woman stopped taking her medicine.

Health literacy
Evidence to practice

Rothman, R. L., D. A. DeWalt, et al. (2004). "Influence of patient literacy on the effectiveness of a primary care-based diabetes disease management program." *JAMA* 292(14): 1711-6.

Objective: To examine the role of literacy on the effectiveness of a comprehensive disease management program for patients with diabetes.

Conclusions: Literacy may be an important factor for predicting who will benefit from an intervention for diabetes management. A diabetes disease management program that addresses literacy may be particularly beneficial for patients with low literacy, and increasing access to such a program could help reduce health disparities.

How to teach with booklets, pamphlets and tearsheets

Booklets, pamphlets, and tear sheets provide information, but only if the learner can read, understand, and apply the contents. Patients and families are often too stressed to focus, read, and learn from a piece of paper. Even if the learner is very motivated, material is learned best through interaction. Printed information that can be referred to at home to guide self-care is essential, especially when self-care skills are complex. Choose the teaching tool most appropriate for the learner's needs.

Handouts don't teach. People teach.

Always discuss booklets, pamphlets, and tear sheets with the learner.

Here are two ways to use a booklet, pamphlet, or tear sheet:

- Give the handout to the learner, ask him or her to read it, and say when you'll be back to discuss it, or

- Go through the handout together. This is best if the learner:
  - has questionable reading skills
    or
  - is very stressed.

- When you discuss the handout with the learner:
  - If there is a space, put the patient's name and the date on the top of the handout. This helps learners recognize the information is important and personal.

  - Give the learner a pen for writing notes or underlining.

  - Use a highlighter to emphasize important information. As you review the contents together, highlight content that is especially important for this learner. This individualizes the handout to your learner.

  - Watch and listen to the learner during this review. Answer questions or concerns as they come up. Clarify difficult concepts and discuss essential points. Tie new information into the learner's knowledge and lifestyle.

  - Ask the learner questions to verify that he or she has learned the key points.

If your learner speaks a language other than yours, and you use a handout in the learner's language, follow the same steps using an interpreter and an English copy of the handout.

Active involvement
Evidence to practice

Johnson, A., J. Sandford, et al. (2006). "Written and verbal information versus verbal information only for patients being discharged from acute hospital settings to home." The Cochrane Database of Systematic Reviews.

Objectives: To determine the effectiveness of providing written health information in addition to verbal information for patients and/ or significant others being discharged from acute hospital settings to home.

Conclusions: This review recommends the use of both verbal and written health information when communicating about care issues with patients and/or significant others on discharge from hospital to home. The combination of verbal and written health information enables the provision of standardized care information to patients and/ or significant others, which appears to improve knowledge and satisfaction.

A frequently asked question

Our clinic appointments are 14 minutes long! How can I take time to teach?

This is not unusual. It is rare in today's health care system to have large blocks of time for teaching. The solution is to teach efficiently and effectively in the time you have.

This applies to health care providers in every setting:

- Take full advantage of teachable moments.
- Involve and individualize.
- Teach in brief, informal interactions imbedded in conversations.
- While you're having the discussion, highlight the most important points on a booklet or tear sheet for the learner to refer to at home.

How to teach with posters and flip cards

Use posters and flip cards to present simple concepts and to summarize teaching. Both are good ways to display illustrations of body parts or desired behaviors.

For example, a table-top sized set of flip cards on a disease process, such as asthma, can be nearby when having a conversation with the learner. You can use it to illustrate a concept such as how a normal lung looks different than a lung during an asthma attack.

If you have a lot of patients who seek antibiotics to treat viral infections, consider putting up a poster that says antibiotics don't work against viruses and are not always appropriate. Refer to it when a patient asks you for a prescription to treat the flu.

If you frequently walk patients up and down a specific hall after surgery, consider hanging posters along the way that announce distances ("You're half way down the hall already!") or benefits of exercise ("Walking gets the gut moving!"). These can provide topics for discussion, reinforce teaching, and distract from discomfort.

How to teach with a video

Videos and DVDs may be shown on a single player or broadcasted on closed circuit televisions.

Most learners are familiar with watching television. This will make it both easier and more difficult to teach with videotapes. Easier, because it is familiar. More difficult because learners are used to high quality, entertaining productions. Their expectations for videos may be quite high. Keep this in mind if you plan to make your own videos.

Choose teaching videos that:

- Are between 5 and 20 minutes long
- Role model desired behaviors
- Use clear, direct, accurate language
- Keep text on the screen long enough to be read
- Address real-life situations
- Are culturally appropriate

- Show people that look like your learners
- Emphasize what to do instead of what not to do
- Are at the right pace (slower for older learners, faster for adolescents)

Before you show the video, give the learner a paper and pen to take notes and tell the learner the following:

- Identify the purpose of the video and how the learner will benefit from it.
- Point out what to look for in the video, with cues to help the learner know when this information appears. For example, "After the baby cries, watch how the mom sets up the breastfeeding pump."

After the video, come back into the room to discuss it and answer any questions.

A quote to ponder

Before showing the videotape, the nurse explained the purpose of the videotape and why the information was important, identified specific learning outcomes to be met from viewing the videotape, and described key points to remember.

Following the videotape, the nurse returned to the clinic waiting area, reviewed the content, and provided an opportunity for patients to ask questions.

— Oermann, 2003, page 153

How to teach without a handout

No matter how wonderful your source, not every topic taught has a handout available in every language. Sometimes you have to teach without a handout.

Don't worry if you don't have a handout. Paper doesn't teach. People do.

The simplest solution:

1. Give the learner a pen and blank paper.

2. Ask the learner to take written notes or draw instructional pictures as you teach.

3. Teach in conversation.

4. When you're done, have the learner teach it all back to you, so you can be sure the information is correct and complete.

Advantage: Learning is enhanced through action. The act of writing actually helps the learner understand and remember the information. Both teaching it back to you and doing the skill reinforce the learning.

Keep in mind that about 20% of all adults in the United States have trouble reading and writing. If you find your learner is resistant to taking notes, he or she may not be able to read or write. Individualize your teaching to the needs of the learner through drawings or audio tapes. Tape the teaching session so your learner can play it back, as needed.

If you are teaching a self-care skill with several steps, another tool is photography. As the learner practices the skill, take a digital photo of each step. Upload the photos to the computer, print them, lay them out in order, add captions, and the learner has a personalized instruction sheet.

Advantage: The learner not only has a guide to use at home, but also proof that he or she was able to perform the skill successfully.

Handouts don't teach, people do Evidence to practice

Crilly, M. and A. Esmail (2005). "Randomized controlled trial of a hypothyroid educational booklet to improve thyroxine adherence." *British Journal of General Practice* 55(514): 362–8.

332 adults who had been prescribed thyroxine for hypothyroidism were allocated to either a group that was posted [mailed] a hypothyroid booklet addressing lay health beliefs or to a group that received usual care.

Conclusion: Brief intervention with an educational booklet has no influence on thyroxine adherence or health in patients with primary hypothyroidism. These findings do not support the routine distribution of health educational materials to improve medication adherence.

How to teach with the internet

As a health care professional, you cannot ignore the impact of the Internet. The public accesses health information from computers and telephones regularly. Newly diagnosed patients use the Internet to learn more about their illnesses, frustrated patients use it to find clinical trials and isolated patients use it for social networking.

Since the goal of patient and family education is to enhance self-care, and patients use the Internet to better take care of themselves, its use should be supported. The most direct way to support Internet use is to teach them how to find appropriate and timely information. Here are tips from the MedlinePlus Guide to Healthy Web Surfing, http://www.nlm.nih.gov/medlineplus/healthywebsurfing.html

- Consider the source. Use recognized authorities.

- Know who is responsible for the content. Does the site identify the author?

- Be a cyberskeptic. Quackery abounds on the Web.
- Look for the evidence. Rely on medical research, not opinion.
- Look for the latest information.
- Is the information current?
- Beware of bias. Who pays for the site?
- Protect your privacy. Health information should be confidential. If there is a registration form, notice what types of questions you must answer before you can view content. If you must provide personal information (such as name, address, date of birth, gender, mother's maiden name, credit card number) you should refer to their privacy policy to see what they can do with your information.
- Consult your health professional.

Here are some other sites you might refer your learners to:

- FAQ: National Library of Medicine Guide to Finding Health Information http://www.nlm.nih.gov/services/guide.html
- Evaluating Health Information http://www.nlm.nih.gov/medlineplus/evaluatinghealthinformation.html
- A Consumer's Guide to Taking Charge of Health Information, Harvard School of Public Health, http://www.health-insight.harvard.edu/

- How to Evaluate Health Information on the Internet: Questions and Answers, National Cancer Institute, http://www.cancer.gov/cancertopics/factsheet/Information/internet

- Finding Reliable Health Information Online, National Human Genome Research Institute, http://www.genome.gov/11008303

Teaching with the internet
Evidence to practice

Fox, S. (2006). Online Health Search 2006. Washington, DC, Pew Internet & American Life Project. http://www.pewinternet.org/PPF/r/190/report_display.asp

Most Internet users start at a search engine when looking for health information online. Very few check the source and date of the information they find. Eighty percent of American Internet users, or some 113 million adults, have searched for information on at least one of seventeen health topics.

Most Internet users start at a general search engine when researching health and medical advice online. Just 15% of health seekers say they "always" check the source and date of the health information they find online, while another 10% say they do "most of the time."

Three-quarters of health seekers say they check the source and date "only sometimes", "hardly ever"," or "never", which translates to about 85 million Americans gathering health advice online without consistently examining the quality indicators of the information they find. Most health seekers are pleased about what they find online, but some are frustrated or confused.

How to teach with an interpreter

You should use an interpreter whenever the learner speaks a language different from yours. Even if the learner understands some English, he or she may not understand technical terms. To ensure informed consent and patient safety, use an interpreter at all key decision-making points, and during learning needs assessment, teaching self care skills, teaching how to identify problems and how to respond, and evaluation of understanding.

Other cues that an interpreter is needed include if the learner:

- requests or brings an interpreter.
- nods or says "yes" to everything. This may reflect respect or a lack of understanding.
- does not speak your language at his or her home.
- is not able to accurately and clearly teach the content back to you in your language.

Use a trained professional interpreter, either in person or by telephone service. They know how to translate medical terms precisely and in a neutral way. They are trained in health care ethics and confidentiality. Do not use a family member, friend, child, or any untrained person to interpret. If possible, use an interpreter of the same sex, age, cultural group, and social status as the learner.

Before the session, tell the interpreter:

- the content, so the interpreter can ask you questions, clarify terms, and be prepared for what is coming.
- he or she may ask for clarification at any time, and may encourage the learner to ask questions.

During the session:

- Have enough time. Using an interpreter may take 2 to 3 times longer than the same conversation in English.
- Have the interpreter sit or stand next to the learner. You face them, and speak directly to the learner (using "you," not "he" or "she").
- Introduce yourself and the interpreter to the learner.
- Tell the learner the conversation is confidential between the three of you.
- Ask one question at a time, using short sentences. This ensures the interpreter

can repeat what you say accurately.

- Use active verbs.
- Be specific rather than general.
- Avoid medical terms, when possible.
- Use pictures and diagrams, when possible.
- Evaluate understanding at regular intervals, asking the learner to explain back to you what he or she understands.
- Do not say anything you do not want the interpreter to tell the learner.
- Do not delegate any tasks to the interpreter. He or she will only interpret.

After the session:

- Discuss with the interpreter how the discussion went from each of your points of view.
- Discuss what could be improved?

Language services
Real-life example

The emergency room physician was about to discharge the 15-year-old patient. His mother spoke only Spanish, and the boy interpreted her concerns. The complaint was stomach ache; the doctor could find nothing wrong and prescribed Maalox.

The hospital interpreter walked by and offered to ask the mom if she had any other questions. The doctor hesitated, but let the interpreter do this. The mom told the interpreter she found empty spray cans in the boy's room, and she was afraid he was going to die from an overdose of inhalants, so she brought him into the emergency room.

Either the boy did not interpret correctly, or she was uncomfortable saying her concerns through him.

Language services
Evidence to practice

American Institutes for Research (2005). *A Patient-Centered Guide to Implementing Language Access Services in Healthcare Organizations.* 2008.

With growing concerns about racial, ethnic, and language disparities in health and health care and the need for healthcare systems to accommodate increasingly diverse patient populations, language access services (LAS) have become more and more a matter of national importance.

The Office of Minority Health has sponsored the development of A Patient-Centered Guide to Implementing Language Access Services in Healthcare Organizations to help healthcare organizations implement effective LAS to meet the needs of their limited English proficient (LEP) patients, thereby increasing their access to health care.

LAS are especially relevant to racial and ethnic disparities in health care. A report by the Institute of Medicine (IOM) on racial and ethnic disparities in health care documented through substantial research that minorities, as compared to their White American counterparts, receive lower quality of care across a wide range of medical conditions, resulting in poorer health outcomes and lower health statuses. The research conducted by the IOM showed that language barriers can cause poor, abbreviated, or erroneous communication, poor decision making on the part of both providers and patients, or ethical compromises. The implementation of appropriate LAS in healthcare settings can serve to:

- Increase access to care
- Improve quality of care, health outcomes, and health status
- Increase patient satisfaction
- Enhance or ensure appropriate resource utilization

Culture and language
Evidence to practice

Flores, G., J. Rabke-Verani, et al. (2002). "The importance of cultural and linguistic issues in the emergency care of children." *Pediatric Emergency Care* 18(4): 271-284.

PubMed was used to perform a literature search (using 17 search terms) of all articles on culture, language, and the emergency care of children published in English or Spanish from 1966 to 1999.

Conclusions: Not appreciating the importance of culture and language in pediatric emergencies can cause lots of problems, including difficulties with informed consent, miscommunication, inadequate understanding of diagnoses and treatment by families, dissatisfaction with care, preventable morbidity and mortality, unnecessary child abuse evaluations, lower quality of care, clinician bias, and ethnic disparities in prescriptions, analgesia, test ordering, and diagnostic evaluations.

How to teach a group

Many think you can save teaching time by teaching patients with the same diagnosis or treatment in a group, rather than individually. This would allow you to teach the same content once instead of once per learner.

But keep in mind the most efficient and effective way to teach adults is to involve them in the process and individualize the teaching. This means you need to create a class that consists of a series of interactive exercises that help the learners experience the content. The instructor decides what the learners need to do to learn. This shifts the focus from the instructor to the adult learner.

If you want learners to remember and use the information, teach half as much content in twice the time. At least half of the class time should be spent with learners speaking to one another in pairs or small groups.

Involving and individualizing to a group takes a special set of skills and a good deal of preparation. You do not create a lesson plan, you design a class. Ask "what do they need to do to learn this topic?" not "what do they need to learn?" It takes about three hours of preparation for every one hour of class time. You decide the objective and choose the appropriate point or points that fit the class timeframe. Here are the steps to teaching groups, adapted from Vella (2002):

- Find out what the members of the group want and need to learn. Ask them to write their questions, or start the class with a discussion of what they want to get out of the session. Find out what skills they want, and why. Identify the common themes, and teach from there.

- Make sure your learners feel safe and comfortable. Set doable objectives, create an accepting atmosphere, recognize efforts, and acknowledge success. Ensure confidentiality within the group. Speaking in small groups feels safer than in front of the whole group. Have the learners discuss a question related to the content in pairs, then have a few pairs share their answers with the whole group. For example, if you are teaching a class to newly diagnosed diabetics, ask them to share, in pairs, what concerns them most about having diabetes. Then ask for volunteers to share, with the whole group, what they discussed.

- Establish relationships to promote dialogue. Start with clear expectations. Begin the session with introductions. Listen to and respect the participants. Learners should also respect others in the group, and tolerate differences.

- Move from small to big, slow to fast, easy to hard. Connect the content to real life. Decide what information the learners need to perform the task. Create activities that build on one another to process information, teach this skill, and address the feelings the situation brings up. Promote success early on to build confidence and self-efficacy. Repeat facts, skills, and attitudes until they are learned.

- Begin with experience, then reflection. Skills are learned by putting information into practice. Have the class do something relevant to the content they are to learn, then think and talk about it. Plan breaks to give them time to reflect on the implications.

- Give the learners control. Offer learners choices. Be clear whether you are asking them for suggestions or offering them decision-making choices. Help them make connections with their own experiences. Give them opportunities for self-assessment and help them establish their own learning goals.

- Teach using ideas, feelings, and actions.

Create interactive activities that involve movement, feelings, and a range of senses. These can be done individually or in small groups. Be creative and use lots of different media. It can involve responding to a story, watching a video, reading a list of quotes and choosing a favorite, exploring medical equipment, or solving a problem. Have learners practice a self-care skill.

- Teach what is really useful to the learner right now. Invite the learners to choose what they find most relevant and decide how they will learn it. Apply what is learned right away and connect the learning tasks to real life. Engage the learners in discovering how the information applies to their lives to solve real-life problems. Brainstorm all the ways to respond to an issue. Refer them to relevant resources they can access when the class is over. A good, comprehensive handout can provide all the content you might have presented in an old-style lecture.

- Encourage team work. Create activities that promote collaboration and build relationships. Include everyone in activities. Adults learn in small group conversations.

- Engage them in the process. Adults learn by doing.

- Include an element of accountability. Teach what you say you will teach.

Learners must demonstrate what they have learned. Ask them how and when they will use the new information at home. What behaviors will they change as a result of this learning? Find out what was useful to learners and what they suggest should be changed. Use that feedback to improve your next group teaching.

How would a class that is not a lecture and a slide show look? It would be a series of activities done by the participants, facilitated by the leader. For example, if the class purpose is to encourage participants to exercise, here are some questions the activities might center around:

- What does it mean to be fit? What are signs that a person is not physically fit?

- What sort of physical activities did you enjoy when you were young?

- What could you do now to build your strength?

- What kind of aerobic activity do you like to do?

- What physical activity will you add to your life, starting tomorrow? How often will you do it? How long will you do it for?

Norris (2003) offers these tips to design the group session activities:

- Don't ask questions that ask the learner to repeat information you just taught them.

- Don't ask a question if you know the

answer. Ask questions that only the learner can answer. These are questions that connect the content to the learner's experience, such as, "describe a time when you . . ."

- Ask open-ended questions that ask the learner to think, such as:
  - Give an example of . . .
  - What would you add to this list, and why?
  - What do you think of?
  - What was the most valuable part of...
  - What do you need to ask to make this clear?
  - How can you remember this?
  - How will this information help you?
  - Name one thing you can change.
- Group activities should start with two to four people, then move to the larger group. Mix up the pairings to keep the energy fresh.
- When asking for findings the whole group will hear, ask for volunteers, wait five full seconds, and someone will speak up. Sample only two or three responses, then move on to the next activity.
- Activities should ground the topic in the learner's lives, provide new information, have the learners do something with the

information, and guide learners to apply this information in the future.

- Use activities that actively involve the learners, whether they are sitting or moving around the room.

  - Put quotes on the walls on posters. Ask participants to stand under the quote that speaks to them right now. Ask the participants under each quote to introduce themselves to one another and explain their choice. Ask for a volunteer from the group to share with the large group the quote and its personal meaning. Sample two or three responses, then move on to the next activity.

  - Have participants create a mind map.

  - Put stickers or colored markers at each table. Encourage participants to personalize their handouts.

  - Have learners write on a postcard a goal they want to accomplish related to the group's topic. Have them address the cards to themselves. After an appropriate time (weeks to months), mail these cards to the learners with an encouraging comment.

An old-fashioned lecture may have allowed you to present more content than in this dialogue approach, but the goal is not transferring information, it is changing health behaviors.

Information can be given in a handout. The involvement and interaction of this group session design is more likely to help the learner internalize the information and apply it. This will ultimately help improve health outcomes.

A quote to ponder

Teachers do not empower adult learners; They encourage the use of the power that learners were born with.

— Vella, 2002, page 10

Evaluating understanding

Teaching and learning are not the same. Just because we've taught something well does not mean anything was learned. What the learner knows and can apply is more important than any handout we give or anything we say. It is more useful to document evaluation of understanding than it is to document what we taught.

This conversation does not evaluate understanding:

Health care professional:
Do you understand?

Patient:
Yes.

Health care professional:
Do you have any questions?

Patient:
No.

Health care professional:
Are you ready to go home?

Patient:
Yes.

This conversation provides no evidence that the teaching was effective. And yet, this is often the conversation that precedes the charted, *"Patient verbalizes understanding."*

Would you document under *"temperature"* on a flow sheet the word *"fever"* instead of the thermometer reading?

Similarly, asking, *"Can you do this?"* and getting a *"yes"* in response does not provide evidence that the learner can do the task correctly and independently.

It doesn't matter what you taught. It only matters what the learner knows.

Two ways to effectively evaluate understanding are through "explain it to me" (teach back) and "show me" (return demonstration).

Explain it to me *(teach back)*

Ask:

- Tell me what you know about . . .
- How would you explain that to . . .
- How would you know if . . .
- Show me how you would . . .
- What would you do if . . .
- Who would you call if . . .

For example, ask the learner how he or she would explain the diagnosis to a family member. Or, ask the learner to describe signs of trouble, and how he or she would respond. Or, if you taught using flip cards, turn to a picture and ask the learner to explain it to you.

Show me *(return demonstration)*

Here's the process for evaluating understanding through return demonstration. Document the learner's progress every step of the way so other team members can pick up teaching where you left off.

1. Prepare the learner. Tell him or her why you're teaching this skill and what you expect from the learner.

2. Show the learner how you do it. Perform the skill with the learner watching, describe what you are doing, and explain why you are doing it.

3. Have the learner practice steps in the skill. The learner may ask for clarification of details and express feelings about the process. Provide encouragement, give tips, and guide the learner into correct performance. Provide rationales as needed.

4. Have the learner repeat the skill, with your feedback, until he or she expresses comfort doing it, and you are confident the learner can perform the skill correctly.

5. Have him or her perform an independent return demonstration.

6. With hours or days in between, have the learner complete at least three unassisted, accurate return demonstrations.

    a. The first return demonstration shows the learner can do the skills.

    b. The second demonstrates the learner can recall the skills over time.

    c. By the third, something may go wrong, such as a break in sterile technique. This will let you evaluate the learner's problem-solving skills.

Both teach back and return demonstration reinforce learning and enhance later recall, by actively involving the learner in the process.

This gives you the opportunity to evaluate skills and reteach when necessary. Evaluate some understanding each day that you interact with the patient and family. Share your finding with the rest of the health care team through documentation. This allows them to pick up teaching where you left off. By spreading education over time and across the disciplines, the teaching done at the time of discharge becomes more of a review than a cramming session.

If your learner does not speak the same language as you, be sure to get an interpreter to evaluate understanding. Since language can create a barrier to effective communication, it is even more important that the learner teach back and return demonstrate essential information and skills.

A quote to ponder

Nothing is so simple that it cannot be misunderstood.

— Freeman Teague

Evaluation of understanding
Real-life example

When scheduling patients for endoscopies, we tell them not to eat breakfast the morning of the exam.

The surgeon started the endoscopy on a farmer, and found he had to irrigate and pump, irrigate and pump, and could not see anything. Upset, he said to the patient, "I thought we told you not to eat any breakfast this morning!"

"Honest, Doc," the patient replied, "I didn't eat no breakfast. All I had was a banana and a cup of coffee."

Evaluation of understanding
Evidence to practice

Paterson, B., B. Kieloch, et al. (2001). "They never told us anything': Postdischarge instruction for families of persons with brain injuries." *ARN: Association of Rehabilitation Nurses* 26(2): 48-53.

This article reports on an analysis of why some families of survivors of traumatic brain injury (TBI) do not perceive that they were prepared for the post-discharge experience, despite discharge planning and teaching by rehabilitation hospital staff and third-party insurance adjusters.

Findings are presented of a research study involving single interviews with seven families of survivors of TBI and interviews with four focus groups of healthcare professionals and third-party insurance adjusters who had cared, or were currently caring, for the injured person.

Most family members did not recall being taught about what to expect or the resources available to them. Healthcare professionals and insurance adjusters, however, stated that extensive discharge planning and multidisciplinary teaching conferences with patients and their families had been held before the patients were discharged. Reasons for such a discrepancy in perceptions are suggested. Implications of these findings for healthcare professionals who conduct discharge teaching in rehabilitation facilities are identified.

Evaluation of understanding
Real-life example

A nurse reviewed bone marrow suppressive effects of chemotherapy with a mom and her 6-year-old daughter with leukemia. The nurse had assessed that the mom had done some research on her own and understood the information quite well. So the nurse spoke to the mom in fairly sophisticated terms, then stopped periodically to summarize in simpler terms for the child.

After a few minutes the child asked the nurse, in a tone of complete exasperation, if she would please use proper names when speaking to her. The girl reported she was quite aware that she "had platelets rather than cells that help your blood clot" and "white blood cells rather than infection-fighting cells." "After all, I'm a 6-year-old!"

The nurse learned there is a difference between developmentally appropriate education and age-appropriate education.

Learning barriers

There are no learning barriers. Only teaching challenges.

Once we decide a patient has a learning barrier, we unwittingly create a teaching barrier. If we think a patient whose primary language is not the same as ours has a "learning barrier," it sets up subconscious walls. We think this barrier will make it hard for us to teach this patient. It will take more work and more time. Our educational efforts may not be successful. But it's not our fault that he has a barrier to learning. We did our best.

Don't look at learning barriers as problems, but as cues that help you better individualize teaching.

Frustration

Sometimes when providing patient and family education, you find the learner is not accepting your teaching, either passively through politeness, or actively through argument or rejection. Or the learner seems upset, uninterested, or confused. You may find you are repeating the same information several times because you are not getting through. Or the learner can't or won't perform skills or apply knowledge. Your first clue that this is happening may be that uncomfortable feeling . . . you are getting frustrated.

If your teaching isn't getting through, frustration is your red flag.

Frustration means what you are doing is not working.

Frustration means you need to better individualize your teaching.

So stop. Go back to assessment. Ask yourself if your goals are the learner's goals, if you're making assumptions, and if the learner believes he or she can do it.

Adults have life experience, and their points of view are a result of all that came before. You may discover the learner does not believe what you assume he believes. You may discover the learner's goals for treatment are not the same as your goals. You may discover the learner is physically unable to perform the skills.

Listen for the learner's cues of discomfort, resistance, misunderstanding, or confusion. Ask questions. Find out what aspect of your learner's point of view is incompatible to your approach. Discover the source of the problem, and adjust your teaching and care plan as necessary. Negotiate, as necessary.

Patient-centered care
Evidence to practice

Russell, S., J. Daly, et al. (2003). "Nurses and 'difficult' patients: negotiating non-compliance." *Journal of Advanced Nursing* 43(3): 281-7.

Aim: The aim of this discussion paper is to build on the critical nursing literature to offer an alternative to the interventions commonly directed at patients who do not follow health care advice. This alternative approach locates patients within their social context and focuses on those who adapt health care advice to fit with their beliefs, life situation and circumstances. The aim is to encourage nurses to learn about how health care treatments affect patients' lives, and not merely their health.

Conclusion: A patient-centered approach involves transferring power and authority away from health care professionals and towards patients. We encourage nurses to take a leadership role by changing the way in which health care is delivered towards a focus on patients' lives. Learning about patients' lives may assist nurses to offer health information to patients that is more relevant and, therefore, more useful.

A quote to ponder

People don't resist change.   They resist being changed.

— Peter Senge

The patient education process

The ultimate goal of patient and family education is to improve health outcomes. The process is both simple and sophisticated.

There are two levels to patient education, but they don't occur in order.

1. Teaching information and skills.
2. Helping the learner apply these new skills to his or her life.

The first level is information sharing. The learner needs information and skills that he or she did not have before.

The second level is coaching behavior change. Having information alone is not enough to change health outcomes. Books, papers, computers can all provide information. Education is the process of internalizing that information, applying that information, and changing behaviors to accommodate to this new health status.

For example, a learner who understands calories, nutrients, and activity does not automatically lose weight. This information has to be internalized and applied to have an effect, and to change health outcomes.

Applying these new skills involves personal change. Butterworth (2008) described ways we thought we could help people change:

- Give them insight. If you can just make people see, they will change.
- Give them knowledge. If people just know enough, they will change.
- Give them skills. If you can just teach people how to change, they will do it.
- Give them a hard time. If you can just make people feel badly or afraid enough, they will change.

But we now know these methods, based on the medical model, don't work very well. Our old ways are not very good at making patients do what we say. Our challenge has shifted from finding the perfect medicine, to getting patients to take their medicines as prescribed. Our challenge has shifted from finding a good diagnostic test, to getting patients to take these tests to diagnose diseases early so we can optimize positive outcomes.

Health care is now evolving from this medical model to patient and family centered care. McEwen and Flowers, 2003, describe how this shift impacts the approach to patient and family education.

The medical model approach believes medical knowledge is the truth; everything else is lay belief. The job of experts is to fix the problem, and tell ignorant patients what is best for them. They assume health behavior will change once patients receive correct and relevant medical information. These health care providers would prescribe a treatment and expect appropriate follow-through by the patient. If it doesn't work, the patient was non-compliant. The intervention was appropriate. It was the patient's fault it didn't work.

Those with the patient-centered approach believe there are multiple realities. The point of view of the health care provider is different from that of the patient. They respect the physical, mental, and spiritual aspects of patients and families and recognize that health exists in a social context. They explore what is best for patients by providing relevant and realistic information. They tailor interventions to the patient's context. The process is interactive. If the treatment doesn't work, something needs to be adjusted.

Our old medical model approach is easier to do. It is black and white, right and wrong. The expert-lay relationship is clear. However, health care providers do not have the power or authority to make competent patients do as they say. When we ignore this fact we don't understand the poor compliance, and we are frustrated by poor health outcomes.

The patient-centered approach is not just black and white; it brings in the whole rainbow. Patients come to us with their life experiences, their points of view, and their preferences. Many variables need to be assessed and weighed. We share power with the patients. Providing health care in this framework requires different skills.

Helping the learner apply new information and skills to his or her life is called coaching. It is the method by which the health care provider helps the patient identify personal goals and transition from old to new behaviors to meet those goals. This takes involving the learner in the process and individualizing education to the learner to a new level. One tool of health coaching is motivational interviewing.

Huffman (2008) defines health coaching as including:

- listening for the patient's agenda
- using the patient's goals to guide safe, collaborative mutual goals
- providing information
- guiding the patient through self-discovery to promote change that improves outcomes

Botelho (2004) provides six steps to negotiate a behavior change. They move patients through the stages of change, from not thinking about change, to thinking about it, to preparing for it, to taking action, and to maintaining that action.

They are:

1. Build a partnership
2. Negotiate an agenda
3. Assess resistance and motivation
4. Enhance mutual understanding
5. Implement a plan
6. Follow through

The partnership is built through listening, affirming, and empathizing with the patient. Uncover the patient's agenda and mutually establish a goal. Then help the patient see the difference between where he or she is now and where he or she wants to be. Help the patient devise a plan to reach the goal.

The health care provider does this without arguing or trying to convince the patient to change. The process is to roll with resistance, rather than hitting it head on. This is done through asking the right open ended questions at the right time, and coaching the patient toward meeting his or her own goals.

Any patient can tell you why a change, like stopping smoking cigarettes, is good. The key is to find out why that patient is not doing it. Help the patient identify personal advantages of not changing, and the disadvantages of changing. Help the patient recognize how his or her behaviors don't support the goals.

Here are some questions that can help the patient through this self-discovery process.

1. Find out what the patient wants.

   - What do you want?
   - What do you hope to achieve?
   - What do you most want to change?
   - What are your concerns?
   - What bothers you most?
   - Tell me what you're most distressed about.
   - Why do you feel that way?

2. Raise doubt. Help the patient perceive the risks and problems with current behavior.

   - What would happen if you didn't make any changes?
   - What choices do you have?

3. Tip the balance. Help the patient realize current behavior does not support personal goals. Help the patient come up with the personal risks of not changing. Help the patient come up with reasons to stay the same. Strengthen the patient's belief he or she can change current behavior.

   - How does doing that get you closer to your goal?
   - Why would you want to keep the old behavior?
   - Why wouldn't you want to move to the new behavior?

- What's getting in your way?
- What part of this is hardest for you?

4. Make a plan. Help the patient decide the best course of action to take.

   - What behavior would you like to change at this time?
   - What option are you most likely to actually do?

5. Take action. Help the patient to take steps toward change.

   - What are you going to do?
   - How are you going to do it?
   - How will you know it is working?

Coach the patient through developing his or her own personal plan, and with specific measurable objectives. Follow-up, and work with the patient to adjust the plan over time. Any movement toward healthier behaviors is progress.

Helping a person change behaviors takes time. That is why it is essential to work with the health care team across the continuum of care. Long-term improvements in health outcomes require more than one teaching encounter.

How far you can take your education is determined by:

- the learner's understanding of the information

- the learner's motivation to change behaviors
- your coaching skills
- the time you have to coach the learner through behavior change
- your collaboration with the health care team across the continuum of care

Change is a process. Be patient.

Coaching
Real-life example

A mom brought her infant into the emergency department after he stopped breathing for a short time after getting caught between two couch pillows. Fortunately, the infant had no apparent lasting damage from the incident.

The nurse asked why the infant was sleeping on the couch, where there was a risk of falling. The mom replied that was where the infant always slept. When the nurse asked if the child had a crib, the mom responded, with great emotion, that she would never put her child in a crib. When the nurse assessed further, she discovered the mom refused to use a crib because she did not want her child to die of crib death.

A quote to ponder

Whether you believe you can do a thing or not, you are right.

— Henry Ford

Self-efficacy

A learner with a new diagnosis is suddenly faced with new challenges. New self-care behaviors need to be learned and incorporated into daily life. It can be overwhelming. Sometimes, the emotional response to these new responsibilities is, "I can't do it."

This belief can, actually, keep the learner from doing it.

Self-efficacy is the learner's perceptions about his or her confidence to perform a particular action. It is specific. For example, a competent, experienced mom may have very low self-efficacy relating to her ability to give her baby daily injections.

When a learner has difficulty applying a self-care skill, but it does not appear to be related to ability or knowledge, assess self-efficacy. Ask the learner:

- How confident are you, on a scale of 1 to 10, that you can . . .

- How confident are you, on a scale of 1 to 10, that you will . . .

1 is low, 10 is high. If the learner's score is under 7 for a specific skill, it indicates a lack of confidence that could interfere with the application of that skill.

If the learner's score is under 7, find out why. Ask the learner what is needed to raise that score. Does the learner need more practice? Does the learner have unanswered questions? What is the learner not sure of? What might the learner need help or support with? What does the learner need to get some experience and gain confidence?

The response will help you design an intervention. There are four ways to increase self-efficacy:

- Skills mastery
- Modeling
- Reinterpretation of physiological signs
- Social persuasion

Skills mastery

If the task is overwhelming, break the task down into doable pieces (Lorig, 1996). Success in one step of the task will build confidence. When each step is mastered, add another step. Ultimately, self-efficacy will increase and the skill will be performed.

One example of this is the Alcoholics Anonymous promise not to drink today. It may be overwhelming to commit to never drinking again, but one day is doable.

Another example: A patient is asked for a confidence level that he can remember to take all the prescribed medicines on time. If the score is below 5, ask the learner what is needed to raise that score. It may be the patient just gets busy with life and forgets. Does the patient need a memory aid, such as a medicine reminder box with an alarm?

Modeling

It may help to see someone else, just like the learner, succeeding. Introduce the learner to others with the same problem. Match the model to the learner by age, sex, ethnicity, and socio-economic status, if possible. Do not use super-achievers as role models.

For example, a parent of a child with a new tracheostomy may be overwhelmed with the responsibility of maintaining the child's airway. Seeing another parent confidently succeed can help raise the self-efficacy score.

If finding a match is difficult within your patient population, there may be an Internet support group that offers appropriate role models. Any teaching media you offer, such as booklets or videos, should use models the learner can identify with.

Reinterpretation of physiological signs

If the learner engages in behaviors you consider irrational, find out what belief is behind that behavior. Ask,

"If you change that behavior, what are you afraid might happen?" or

"When you think about (disease or new behavior), what do you think of?" or

"Why don't you change that behavior?"

For example, a patient with a chronic illness may be depressed, but perceive the fatigue associated with the depression as a symptom of worsening chronic illness. Help the patient understand that if fatigue is a symptom of the illness, resting may help. However, if fatigue is a symptom of depression, exercise, even just walking, may help. This may increase the patient's belief that he or she can increase frequency of exercise.

Social persuasion

Persuasion is a popular way to help people change behaviors, but fear arousal and social support are not very effective at changing core beliefs. They may help for short-term goals.

For example, a health care provider can encourage a patient to do just a little bit more exercise. It needs to be realistic, and just slightly more than the patient's belief of what is possible. This may influence a short-term increase in exercise.

Coaching an increase in self-efficacy may take some detailed assessment and individualized interventions, but it can take the learner to improved health outcomes.

Coaching
Real-life example

A patient in acute pain refuses to take a narcotic. Find out what experiences he has had with narcotics, what he knows about narcotics, how he feels about addiction, and experiences with the pain. Within this context, correct misperceptions and reframe the issue in terms of quality of life. This reorganizes the patient's current knowledge and can help move him to a new understanding.

A frequently asked question

"How do I teach the family if they're not there?"

This situation is common. You know the patient cannot care for himself and will need complex home care. You're ready to teach, but the family members and significant others never come to the facility to be taught!

They may not come in because they have children to care for, a great distance to travel, transportation problems, jobs or responsibilities that take most of their time, or a combination of these. They may have been caring for the patient at home, and are looking at this as a respite. Maybe they can't agree on who will care for the patient. You may never learn why they do not come in.

Here are some possible responses:

- Find out if the family members know you expect them to be part of the patient's health care team. Do they know that part of the treatment includes teaching them how to care for the patient at home?

- Call the significant other or family members. Find out what their expectations are. What are their concerns? Are other care providers involved? Is the person you're waiting to meet with the right person to teach?

- Engage the entire health care team. Does the family call the attending physician for medical updates? Does the social worker or case manager talk to the family? Get them involved in scheduling teaching time with the right learners.

- If the learner can only visit the hospital occasionally, make an appointment to teach. Follow up with a written reminder or phone call. Obtain back up support so you are available to teach.

- If you meet with resistance, return to assessment. Are you trying to meet their learning goals or your teaching goals? Do family members believe they are capable of caring for this patient at home? Should other team members, such as the primary care physician, social worker, or home care nurse take on a bigger role? Do you need to schedule a team meeting to share information about the family and develop a plan?

A quote to ponder

On the average, for every dollar invested in patient education, $3 - 4 were saved.

— Bartlett, 1995, page 89

Are you concerned this education process takes too long?

What is the point of providing health care?

To improve long-term health outcomes.

What has the greatest impact on long-term health outcomes?

After the immediacy of saving lives, self-care behaviors have the greatest impact on long-term health outcomes.

What has the greatest impact on self-care behaviors?

The information and coaching provided by patient and family education.

The brief interventions of health care providers may stop or reverse illness. But it is the responsibility of the patient and family to take measures that maintain that momentary success, by continuing with self-administered medications and treatments, and lifestyle changes.

The time you spend teaching costs less than the complications, medications, hospitalizations, and surgeries you can prevent. Patient and family education saves money only if learning occurs and behaviors change. Both assessment and evaluation of understanding are essential to effective patient and family education, and make good financial sense.

The good news is you are not alone. Patient and family education is the responsibility of every health care provider across the continuum of care.

Collaborate

The behavior changes that patients and families need to make to improve health outcomes range from the very simple (take 81 mg of aspirin each morning) to very complex (self-management of multiple chronic illnesses).

The most effective way to support lasting behavior changes is if all the health care providers working with the patient and family across the continuum of care collaborate.

Patients and families need to understand their role in continuing care, and that optimal health outcomes depend on their collaboration with the health care team. They need to make their goals known, and hold health care providers accountable for education. They should understand they have the right to a clear explanation of:

- What's my problem?
- What do I need to do?
- Why?

Then, health care providers need to understand that every interaction and every conversation with the patient and family contributes to patient and family education. It is the continuous, never-ending process of assessment, teaching, and evaluation of understanding.

Communicate assessments and progress to other members of the health care team along the continuum, to facilitate collaboration and consistency of education. When team members discuss care of a specific patient, include information about patient education (assessment, effectiveness of specific teaching methods, evaluation of understanding). This information should also be communicated through documentation.

Administration and management can influence staff attitudes by providing resources, through policies, competency evaluations, and holding staff accountable for teaching and communicating status of patient education to the rest of the health care team verbally and through documentation.

A quote to ponder

"Patient education is often invisible in management's eyes because it is frequently undocumented, unmonitored, and underappreciated for the skill and experience it demands. The positive impact of effective patient education on health outcomes and costs is not taken into account in day-to-day health care delivery."

— Rankin, Stallings, & London, 2005, page 119.

Communicate the status of patient and family education — document it!

Before you gave a medication to treat pain, would you check the chart to find out when it was given last? Would you check to see the effectiveness of the last prn pain med given, before you decided whether to give an oral or IV med?

So why would you jump into teaching without checking the chart to see what others assessed and found effective?

It may seem we are taking more time by communicating the status of patient education to other members of the team through documentation. But in fact, by coordinating our efforts, we can build on the assessments, teaching, and coaching of others, and have our education reinforced and strengthened across the continuum of care.

Since teaching is almost always done alone with the patient or family, reading what others have documented and documenting your progress minimizes wasted teaching time for everyone on the team. It ensures continuity and reinforcement of teaching without duplication.

It is easy to skip documentation of patient and family education if you see it merely as a regulatory requirement, irrelevant to patient care. Unfortunately, many managers and administrators encourage documentation for this reason, contributing to persistent non-documentation.

Yes, other reasons to document the status of patient and family education include:

— to have a legal record of assessment and evaluation of understanding

— to meet requirements of regulatory agencies such as Joint Commission

— to have data for quality measures and research

— to have evidence for reimbursement from third party payors

However, the most important reason to document the status of patient and family education is to communicate to the other health care team members where teaching left off. This includes other members of the interdisciplinary team within the organization and across the continuum of care.

For example: On three consecutive shifts, three consecutive nurses requested an Asthma Booklet for the same admitted patient. None had documented that they obtained the booklet, nor assessed the family's need for the booklet. Time and resources were wasted, and the family's trust was undermined because it appeared the nurses didn't even talk to one another.

Documentation of education throughout the admission can demonstrate how the patient and family were involved throughout the process and teaching was individualized to their needs. It will provide clear evidence of quality patient-centered and family-centered care.

A frequently asked question

"How do we get our organization's top leadership to see the value of patient education and provide the necessary financial resources?"

Your organization's top leadership probably knows the value of patient and family education. It is one of the highest correlates with patient satisfaction.

On the other hand, top leadership may not understand what is taught, and when and how it is taught. They may not understand that, to be most cost-effective, we need to take advantage of teachable moments. This means we need to maintain an environment that supports readiness to teach and flexibility of time to take advantage when opportunities arise. If staffing is too tightly staffed to allow for spontaneity, teaching opportunities will be missed. Teaching done at the wrong times will be more time consuming and less effective.

Educate top leadership about the importance of patient and family education in terms they understand. Tell them about studies that correlate excellence in patient and family education with cost-effectiveness, patient satisfaction, and low readmissions. Suggest they use patient and family education as a tool to promote and market the organization. It is a low-tech, high-touch customer service that the community appreciates.

How to waste teaching time

- Make assumptions.
- Teach before you know who you are teaching.
- Talk, talk, talk.
- Lecture.
- Don't let the learner interrupt you.
- Listen in a hurry. Make the loudest voice the voice in your head, forming your next statement.
- Ignore or make light of a learner's concerns.
- Teach when the problem isn't a lack of information.

Summary

The key to effective and efficient teaching is to involve the learner in the process, individualize teaching to the needs of the learner, and collaborate teaching with the rest of the health care team across the continuum of care.

- Incorporate patient and family teaching into every interaction with the patient and family. If you are not actively teaching, you are assessing needs or evaluating understanding.

- Involve the learners, identify their specific needs, and individualize your teaching. Set learning goals with patient and family.

- Focus on teaching the behaviors and skills relating to the highest priorities: informed consent, self-care skills, how to recognize problems and know how to respond, and answering questions.

- Teach in two-way conversation. Listen. Ask questions.

- Individualize your teaching by choosing the right teaching tools to meet the learner's needs. When appropriate, provide and review materials that contain detailed information the learner will need to refer to later (booklets, pamphlets, tear sheets, websites, community resources, contact information).

- Evaluate understanding.

- Learn about, listen to, and respect your learner. Tailor interventions to the learner's context.

- Coach the learner through the behavior changes needed to improve health outcomes. Help the learner identify his or her own health goals, decide what actions to take to reach those goals, and follow-up over time, either personally or through others providing continuing care.

- Build on the teaching and assessments of others, and communicate the status of patient education to other members of the health care team through documentation.

If you want to learn more

American Institutes for Research (2005). *A Patient-Centered Guide to Implementing Language Access Services in Healthcare Organizations.* 2008.

Ask Me 3, Partnership for Clear Health Communication. 2006. Good Questions for Patients' Good Health http://www.askme3.org/

Austin, J. and F. London (2008). *How much information do you want?* Workshop on Sudden Unexpected Death in Epilepsy (SUDEP), Rockville, MD, National Institute of Neurological Disorders and Stroke.

Bartlett, E. E. (1995). *Cost-benefit analysis of patient education.* Patient Education and Counseling, 26, 87-91.

Botelho, R. (2004). *Motivational Practice: Promoting healthy habits and self-care of chronic illnesses.* Rochester, NY, MHH Publications.

Butterworth, S. W. (2008). "Influencing Patient Adherence to Treatment Guidelines." *Journal of Managed Care Pharmacy* 14(6) (suppl S-b): S21-S25.

Crilly, M. and A. Esmail (2005). "Randomised controlled trial of a hypothyroid educational booklet to improve thyroxine adherence." *British Journal of General Practice* 55(514): 362–8.

Dass, R. and P. Gorman (1985). *How Can I Help? Stories and reflections on service.* New York City, Alfred A. Knopf.

Doak, C. C., L. G. Doak, et al. (1996). *Teaching patients with low literacy skills.* Philadelphia, J. B. Lippincott Company.

Enslein J, Tripp-Reimer T, Kelley LS, Choi E, McCarty L. *Evidence-based protocol. Interpreter facilitation for persons with limited English proficiency.* Iowa City (IA): University of Iowa Gerontological Nursing Interventions Research Center, Research Dissemination Core; 2001 Apr. 32 p.

Flores, G., J. Rabke-Verani, et al. (2002). "The importance of cultural and linguistic issues in the emergency care of children." *Pediatric Emergency Care* 18(4): 271-284.

Fox, S. (2006). Online Health Search 2006. Washington, DC, Pew Internet & American Life Project. http://www.pewinternet.org/PPF/r/190/report_display.asp

Gerteis, M., S. Edgman-Levitan, et al., Eds. (2002). *Through the Patient's Eyes: Understanding and Promoting Patient-Centered Care*, New Edition, Jossey-Bass.

Herndon, E. and L. Joyce (2004). "Getting the most from language interpreters." *Family Practice Management* (June): 37-40.

Huffman, M. H. (2008). *Health Coaching! A Fresh, New Approach that Enhances Patient-Self Management & Improves Outcomes!* Health Care Education Conference 2008, Tempe, AZ, Health Care Education Association.

Jahraus, D., S. Sokolosky, et al. (2002). "Evaluation of an education program for patients with breast cancer receiving radiation therapy." *Cancer Nursing* 25(4): 266-275.

Johnson, A., J. Sandford, et al. (2006). "Written and verbal information versus verbal information only for patients being discharged from acute hospital settings to home." *The Cochrane Database of Systematic Reviews.*

The Joint Commission. (2003) *The Joint Commission guide to patient and family education* (2nd ed.) Oakbrook, Illinois: Joint Commission Resources.

Keeping, L. (2002). "Self-care, healthcare reform, and their implications to nursing." *Healthcare Management Forum*: 66-72.

Kleinman, A., L. Eisenberg, et al. (1978). "Culture, Illness, and Care: Clinical lessons from anthropologic and cross-cultural research." *Annals of Internal Medicine* 88(2): 251-258.

Logan, P. D., R. A. Schwab, et al. (1996). "Patient understanding of emergency department discharge instructions." *Southern Medical Journal* 89(8): 770-775.

London, F. (2005a). "Moving beyond teaching checklists." Patient Education Update Retrieved 4/12/2009, from http://www.patienteducationupdate.com/2005-10-01/article4.asp

London, F. (2005b). "Three sure things in life: Death, taxes, and no documentation of patient education." *Patient Education Update*(II).

London, F. (2008). "Meeting the challenge: Patient education in a diverse America." *Journal for Nurses in Staff Development.*

London, F. (1999). *No time to teach.* Philadelphia: Lippincott, Williams & Wilkins.

Lorig, K. (1996). *Patient education: A practical approach.* Thousand Oaks, CA, Sage Publications.

McEwen, C., R. Flowers, et al. (2003). *Learner-Centred and Culturally Responsive Patient Education: Drawing on traditions of cultural development and popular education.* Sydney, Australia, Diversity Health Department, Prince of Wales Hospital and University of Technology. 2006. http://www.cpe.uts.edu.au

Norris, J. (2003). *From telling to teaching: A dialogue approach to adult learning.* North Myrtle Beach, SC: Learning by Dialogue.

Oermann, M. H. (2003). "Effects of educational intervention in waiting room on patient satisfaction." *Journal of Ambulatory Care Management* 26(2): 150-8.

Partnership for Clear Health Communication. Ask me 3. Retrieved August 2, 2007, from www.askme3.org

Paterson, B., B. Kieloch, et al. (2001). "'They never told us anything': Postdischarge instruction for families of persons with brain injuries." *ARN: Association of Rehabilitation Nurses* 26(2): 48-53.

Payne, R. K. (2005). *A framework for understanding poverty.* Highlands, TX, Aha! Process Inc.

Pieper, B., M. Sieggreen, et al. (2006). "Discharge Information Needs of Patients After Surgery." *Journal of Wound, Ostomy and Continence Nursing* 33(3): 281-290.

Palazzo, M. O. (2001). "Teaching in crisis. Patient and family education in critical care." *Critical Care Nursing Clinics of North America* 13(1): 83-92.

Rankin, S. H., K. D. Stallings, et al. (2005). *Patient Education in Health and Illness.* Philadelphia, PA, Lippincott Williams & Wilkins.

Rothman, R. L., D. A. DeWalt, et al. (2004). "Influence of patient literacy on the effectiveness of a primary care-based diabetes disease management program." *JAMA* 292(14): 1711-6.

Russell, S., J. Daly, et al. (2003). "Nurses and 'difficult' patients: negotiating non-compliance." *Journal of Advanced Nursing* 43(3): 281-7.

Suhonen, R., H. Nenonen, et al. (2005). "Patients' informational needs and information received do not correspond in hospital." *Journal of Advanced Nursing* 14: 1167-1176.

Taylor, R. (2005). "Addressing barriers to cultural competence." *Journal for Nurses in Staff Development* 21(4): 135-42; quiz 143-4.

Vella, J. (2002). *Learning to Listen, Learning to Teach: The Power of Dialogue in Educating Adults.* New York, Jossey-Bass.

Welch, J. L., M. L. Fisher, et al. (2002). "A cost-effectiveness worksheet for patient-education programs." *Clinical Nurse Specialist* 16(4): 187-182.

Winickoff, J. P., V. J. Hills, et al. (2003). "A smoking cessation intervention for parents of children who are hospitalized for respiratory illness: The Stop Tobacco Outreach Program." *Pediatrics* 111(1): 140-145.

Biography

Fran London's current position as Health Education Specialist at Phoenix Children's Hospital has given her the opportunity to keep up on the research in the field. She has presented workshops and published books, book chapters, and articles on patient education.

She has a BA in Anthropology from Brooklyn College, and a BS in Nursing and MS in Psychiatric Mental Health Nursing from the University of Rochester in New York.

Fran has worked as a staff nurse in pediatrics and psychiatry, inpatient and outpatient; school nurse; and Psychiatric Consultation Liaison Nurse.

Our relationship has just begun with this book. If you have comments, questions, or want to keep up on progress in patient and family education, log on to the website:

www.notimetoteach.com

If you would like to use Twitter to enhance your patient education practice:

- Sign on for a free account at Twitter (www.twitter.com).

- You can access your Twitter account on this website. If you choose to access it on your telephone, it counts as text messages.

- Search #pted to find the latest tweets relating to patient and family education.

- If you want to post information, or a link to an article, website, or abstract relating to patient and family education, include #pted so your post will be found in a search.

- You may also follow Fran London on Twitter at http://twitter.com/franlondon